Put Beg...

ALL AB...

The All Aboard Reading series is espec... ...nning readers. Written
by noted authors and illustrated in full ... books that children really
want to read—books to excite their imagi... ..., expand their interests, make them
laugh, and support their feelings. With fiction and nonfiction stories that are high
interest and curriculum-related, All Aboard Reading books offer something for every
young reade... ...ading series
lets you ch... ...their
growing ab...

Picture Re...
Picture Rea... ...rebus
pictures. A... ...us picture;
on the othe...

Station Sto...
Station Sto... ...Simple words
and big typ... ...cture clues
help childr... ...oughout
the text he... ...step in
developing...

Station Sto...
Station Stop... ...; with help.
Short sente... ...are reading.
Simple plot... ...sion.

Station Sto...
Station Stop... ...h longer text
and harde... ...ic reading
skills. Mor... ...allenging
books.

In additio... ...ers™ (fiction
stories tha... ...rd Science
Readers™... ...cs in
age-appro... ...poems for
readers of... ...here
children p...

All Aboard...

GROSSET & DUNLAP
Published by the Penguin Group
Penguin Group (USA) Inc., 375 Hudson Street, New York, New York 10014, USA
Penguin Group (Canada), 90 Eglinton Avenue East, Suite 700,
Toronto, Ontario M4P 2Y3, Canada
(a division of Pearson Penguin Canada Inc.)
Penguin Books Ltd., 80 Strand, London WC2R 0RL, England
Penguin Group Ireland, 25 St. Stephen's Green, Dublin 2, Ireland
(a division of Penguin Books Ltd.)
Penguin Group (Australia), 250 Camberwell Road, Camberwell, Victoria 3124, Australia
(a division of Pearson Australia Group Pty. Ltd.)
Penguin Books India Pvt. Ltd., 11 Community Centre, Panchsheel Park,
New Delhi—110 017, India
Penguin Group (NZ), 67 Apollo Drive, Rosedale, North Shore 0632, New Zealand
(a division of Pearson New Zealand Ltd.)
Penguin Books (South Africa) (Pty.) Ltd., 24 Sturdee Avenue,
Rosebank, Johannesburg 2196, South Africa

Penguin Books Ltd., Registered Offices:
80 Strand, London WC2R 0RL, England

Photo credits: cover: © Discovery Communications/photo credit: Ron Levine, additional snake
photos: (upper left) © Philippe Clement/Nature Picture Library, (lower left) © DEA/F. BALLANTI/
De Agostini Picture Library/Getty Images, (right) © GK Hart/Vikki Hart/Photodisc/Getty Images;
(bottom) © Gerold & Cynthia Merker/Visuals Unlimited/Getty Images; title page: © Bob Elsdale/
The Image Bank/Getty Images; border (pages 4-48): © Siede Dreis/Photodisc/Getty Images;
page 4: © Discovery Communications/photo credit: Ron Levine; page 5: © Geoff Simpson/
Nature Picture Library; page 6: © Daly & Newton/Riser/Getty Images; page 7: © Niall Benvie/
Nature Picture Library; page 8: © DEA PICTURE LIBRARY/De Agostini Picture Library/
Getty Images; page 9: © Tony Phelps/Nature Picture Library; page 10: © Jim Merli/
Visuals Unlimited/Getty Images; page 11: © Stephen St. John/National Geographic/Getty Images;
page 12: © Barry Mansell/Nature Picture Library; page 13: © Joel Sartore/National Geographic/
Getty Images; page 14: © Norbert Rosing/National Geographic/Getty Images;
page 15: © Norbert Rosing/National Geographic/Getty Images; page 16: © Joel Sartore/
National Geographic/Getty Images; page 17: © Jim Merli/Visuals Unlimited/Getty Images;
page 18: © Rudolf Arndt/Visuals Unlimited/Getty Images; page 19: © Jan Stromme/Stone/
Getty Images; page 21: © Digital Vision/Digital Vision/Getty Images; page 23: © Gerold & Cynthia
Merker/Visuals Unlimited/Getty Images; page 24: (left) © Michael Langford/Gallo Images/
Getty Images, (right) © Barry Mansell/Nature Picture Library; page 25: © Tony Phelps/
Nature Picture Library; page 26: © Martin Harvey/Digital Vision/Getty Images;
page 27: © Martin Harvey/Photographer's Choice RF/Getty Images; page 28: © Tom Brakefield/
Photodisc/Getty Images; page 29: © James Martin/The Image Bank/Getty Images;
page 31: (top) © Gary Bell/Taxi/Getty Images, (bottom left) © Hanne & Jens Eriksen/Nature Picture
Library, (bottom right) © Mike Severns/The Image Bank/Getty Images; page 33: © Frank & Joyce
Burek/Photodisc/Getty Images; page 34: © Guenter Leitenbauer; page 35: © Beverly Joubert/
National Geographic/Getty Images; page 36: © Rod Patterson/Gallo Images/Getty Images;
page 37: © Joel Sartore/National Geographic/Getty Images; page 39: (top) © Edna Barney,
(bottom) © Joel Sartore/National Geographic/Getty Images; page 41: © Joe McDonald/
Visuals Unlimited/Getty Images; page 43: © HERMANN BREHM/Nature Picture Library;
page 44: © Nick Garbutt/Nature Picture Library; page 45: © Peter Blackwell/Nature Picture Library;
page 46: © Miles Barton/Nature Picture Library; page 47: © RainForest Adventures, Inc.;
page 48: © Ken Lucas/Visuals Unlimited/Getty Images

Text copyright © 2009 by Jeff Corwin. All rights reserved. Published by Grosset & Dunlap,
a division of Penguin Young Readers Group, 345 Hudson Street, New York, New York 10014.
ALL ABOARD READING and GROSSET & DUNLAP are trademarks of Penguin Group (USA) Inc.
Printed in the U.S.A.

Library of Congress Control Number: 2009017618
ISBN 978-0-448-45177-0   10 9 8 7 6 5 4 3 2

JEFF CORWIN
SNAKES

◆

Grosset & Dunlap

Hi! I'm Jeff Corwin, and I'm fascinated by snakes! I love all animals, but my favorite are snakes. I've been hooked on them since I was a little kid. Garter snakes, mambas, pythons, rattlers, cobras—they all amaze me!

These are some of my favorite snakes.

A lot of people think snakes are scary, slimy, and dangerous. But that's because they haven't gotten to know snakes like I have. There are definitely some snakes that can be dangerous if they aren't respected. But once you learn more about them, you'll see how amazing they are, too—in so many different ways.

sizing up snakes

Snakes live in all kinds of places—deserts, jungles, forests, prairies, savannahs, underground, and even in the ocean.

The longest snakes are pythons. Reticulated pythons can grow to be as long as thirty feet. That's as long as a school bus! The smallest snakes are thread snakes. The Martinique thread snake grows to just over four inches long. It would take almost one hundred thread snakes placed end to end to be as long as a python!

Some snakes inject *venom* when they bite. Venom is a poisonous liquid. Different snakes have different types of venom. Depending on the snake, the venom may affect the victim's blood, muscles, or nervous system. Snakes inject their venom through sharp teeth called fangs.

There are also many snakes that aren't

venomous. Whether they are venomous or not, snakes usually only harm humans when we bother them. You just have to know which are safe and which aren't— and treat them all with respect.

Cold-blooded animals

Snakes are reptiles. Like all reptiles, snakes are covered with scales. They are also cold-blooded. That means their body temperature changes as the temperature around them changes. When the temperature goes down, their bodies get cool and they slow down. If you see a snake lying on a rock in the sun, it may be trying to get warm so it can start its day. This is called basking.

BASKING

That's a Lot of Babies!

One of the amazing things about snakes is that they give birth to their young in different ways.

Most snakes lay eggs—just like birds. But unlike birds, snakes don't usually take care of their eggs before they hatch. Instead, most mother snakes leave their eggs to hatch on their own.

INDIAN COBRA COILING AROUND ITS EGGS

ADDER GIVING BIRTH TO LIVE YOUNG

Other snakes give birth to live babies. The snakes grow inside the mother until they're ready to come into the world. Many of the snakes that live in the sea and never touch land give birth to live young. So do many snakes that live in trees.

Snakes usually have anywhere between five and forty babies. And you thought having one or two brothers or sisters was annoying. Imagine having forty!

Too Big for Their own skin!

Have you ever touched a snake? Lots of people think snakes feel wet and slimy. In fact, most snakes have smooth, dry skin that feels like plastic or leather.

As a snake grows, its body gets too big for its own skin. When this happens, the snake sheds its outer layer of skin.

To begin shedding, the snake produces a slick liquid under its skin. This makes the snake's colors look dull, and its eyes milky. Next, it rubs its head on a rock or rough piece of wood until the skin begins to tear and come off. Then it slithers over rough ground or through bushes—and crawls right out of its skin! Underneath the old layer of skin is a new

KING SNAKE SHEDDING ITS SKIN

layer that's been growing all along!

If there are snakes where you live, you might be able to find the skin a snake has left behind.

FRESHLY SHED FIVE-FOOT-LONG BLACK SNAKE SKIN

Now that we've learned some neat facts about snakes, let's take a closer look at some of my favorites. Enjoy!

GARTER SNAKE ◇◇◇◇◇◇◇◇◇◇ ◆

Garter snakes are small, slender serpents that won't bite unless threatened. Garter snakes have no venom, but they do produce an offensive smell meant to drive off predators. They're very common and can be found almost anywhere in North America. But they're still fascinating serpents.

Take the red-sided garter snake. To survive the winter, this serpent heads underground to hibernate. (Hibernating is almost like sleeping. Animals escape the chill of winter by resting in underground dens where the temperature doesn't go below zero degrees.)

Sometimes, a garter snake will get caught out in the freezing cold before it can reach a den. When this happens, the water in

the snake's body begins to freeze. That would kill most other animals— including us! But the red-sided garter is special. Almost half of the liquid in its body can turn into ice crystals and it will still be fine—at least for a little while. Brrrr! That's what I call cold-blooded!

RED-SIDED GARTER SNAKE

When hibernation time arrives, it's not always easy to find enough warm, underground shelter. So the snakes share their dens with one another. In Manitoba, Canada, tens of thousands of red-sided garter snakes crowd into only a handful of winter dens.

When the spring comes and the snakes emerge into the warm weather, it's an amazing sight. The ground becomes covered with a thick, coiling, slithering carpet of snakes.

Unfortunately, for years the snakes

RED-SIDED GARTER SNAKES EMERGING

were being killed by cars as they crossed the local highway to get to their dens. So the people of Manitoba put up fences to keep the snakes from slithering onto the road. They also built small tunnels that ran from one side of the highway to the other. Now the snakes use the tunnels to avoid becoming "road-burger."

A CARPET OF RED-SIDED GARTER SNAKES

HOGNOSE SNAKE

You might not think a snake called a hognose could be lovable, but I have a soft spot in my heart for these guys. When I was young, I had a pet hognose snake named Gilda.

Hognose snakes are found mostly in North America. They get their name from their upturned noses, which they use to dig in the ground for their favorite food: toads.

WESTERN HOGNOSE

Like most hognose species, the Madagascar hognose snake has fangs at the rear of its mouth. The fangs come in handy at dinnertime. When a Madagascar hognose snake grabs a toad in its mouth, the toad puffs itself up like a balloon. The toad does this to make itself harder to swallow.

CLOSE-UP OF A HOGNOSE

That's where the fangs come in. The snake bites the toad with its sharp teeth, breaking the toad's skin. The toad deflates and can then be swallowed.

Hognose snakes defend themselves the same way that frogs do. When threatened, these snakes puff themselves up, just like the toad. That's why they have the nickname, puff adder.

The trouble is, this doesn't always work. If the attacker doesn't back off, the hognose rolls over on its back and opens its mouth wide—as if it were dead. It even produces a foul smell from its back end. Many animals won't eat dead meat, so "playing dead" can actually save the hognose's life.

EASTERN HOGNOSE "PLAYING DEAD"

SPITTING COBRA

When threatened, cobras raise their bodies off the ground and flatten their necks into a hood.

SPITTING COBRA

Then there's the spitting cobra, which lives in Africa. If an animal—or human—ignores these warning signs, the spitting cobra has one more trick up its sleeve.

When a venomous snake bites, it squeezes venom from special glands in its head. The liquid squirts through holes near the tips of its fangs and into its attacker or prey. The spitting cobra's fangs are special. They have small holes in them, too, but the holes are in the front of the tooth, not the tip.

A spitting cobra opens its mouth and squeezes venom from its glands. The venom squirts out of the holes, right at the attacker. The spray can travel nearly ten feet!

The spitting cobra aims at the eyes. And believe me, these snakes have great aim. I know because I've had a cobra spit at me. The only thing that kept me from being hit in the eyes was my safety visor. It's a good thing I was wearing one!

MOZAMBIQUE SPITTING COBRA

CORAL SNAKE

Did you know that there are nearly seventy kinds of coral snakes? These highly venomous serpents live in North, South, and Central America. Most are small, but a few species can sometimes grow to nearly five feet long. The coral snake belongs to the same family as the cobra and the mamba. So you won't be surprised to learn that it's venomous, too.

Coral snakes are beautiful creatures, with bands of red, black, and yellow along their slender bodies. They look very similar to milk snakes and king snakes, which aren't venomous. This protects milk and king snakes because predators are fooled into believing they are dangerous coral snakes. This type of protection is called mimicry.

MILK SNAKE

KING SNAKE

CORAL SNAKE

So how can you tell a deadly coral from a harmless milk or king snake? By remembering this old rhyme:

"Red touches black—friend of Jack. Red touches yellow—kill a fellow."

If the snake's red and black bands touch, you're safe. If its red and yellow bands touch, it's a venomous coral—and you need to be very, very careful.

But this doesn't always work—some coral snakes don't follow this rule. So it's best to treat any red, yellow, and black-banded snake with lots of respect.

CORAL SNAKES

AFRICAN CORAL SNAKE

KING COBRA

What would you call a snake that can kill an elephant with a single bite? How about "your majesty?"

The king cobra's bite injects a huge amount of very strong venom into its victim. This makes it one of the deadliest snakes around. Sound scary? It just means you have to treat this royal serpent with extra respect so that it doesn't think you are a threat.

The king cobra gives plenty of warning before it bites. When threatened, it lifts its head high in the air and stares into the eyes of its foe. It flattens its neck into a broad, menacing hood. And it bares its fangs as if to say, "You'd better leave me alone."

The slender, brown or tan king cobra lives in India and Southeast Asia. It normally grows to about fourteen feet in length. But some have been known to grow as long as twenty feet. In fact, this serpent, which feeds mostly on other snakes, is the largest venomous snake on the planet.

KING COBRA

KING COBRA

The king cobra is also special because it is the only snake that builds a nest for its eggs. The mother cobra pulls leaves and twigs around the eggs with her coils. Then she and the father both stand watch, protecting their family-to-be from hungry predators. Now that's what I call royal treatment!

SEA SNAKE

Sea snakes live in the Pacific and Indian Oceans. Most never touch land—they are born, live, and die in the sea. Not surprisingly, they eat mostly fish. But there are some that eat shrimp and crab, and others that only eat fish eggs.

Most sea snakes live near the shore, where they can find food. Others gather by the thousands and drift on the surface of the ocean. Fish are attracted to these floating serpent "islands." When they approach, they're gobbled up by the snakes.

Sea snakes are amazing animals. They can dive hundreds of feet below the surface, and can stay underwater for as long as a few hours. You and I would need an oxygen tank to do that! But sea snakes already have everything they need to survive.

OLIVE SEA SNAKE

ANDED SEA SNAKES

Instead of an oxygen tank, sea snakes have a single, large lung that is perfect for diving. Unlike snakes that live mostly on land, one part of the sea snake's lung is used for storing extra air. On long, deep dives, muscles squeeze the air from this part of the lung to the part used for breathing. It's like the snake has an oxygen tank inside its body!

Instead of flippers, sea snakes have flattened bodies and paddlelike tails that make them great swimmers. Plus, they don't need a scuba mask. Sea snakes have special valves on their nostrils to keep out water. The scales around their mouths are also watertight—except for a valve that opens and closes to let the tongue in and out.

And that's not all. Living in the ocean, these serpents take in a lot of salt that they have to get rid of somehow. The salt is collected in a special organ in the animal's mouth. From there, the salt goes onto the tongue. Then, when the snake flicks its tongue into the water, the salt washes off. Pretty cool, huh?

BANDED SEA SNAKE

BLACK MAMBA

Meet one of the world's most venomous snakes—the black mamba. Black mambas aren't actually black. They're usually brown or gray. They get their name from the dark, blue-black color on the inside of their mouths. You'll want to take my word for this. The only way to see the inside of a black mamba's mouth is to get it mad at you! And you don't want to do that!

When a black mamba feels threatened, it lifts its head high off the ground—like it's standing. The biggest black mambas grow to between twelve and fourteen feet long. And a really large one can lift its head over four feet in the air!

BLACK MAMBAS

Once it raises its head, the black mamba spreads its neck—much like a cobra—and opens its jaws. The black mamba's venom is

BLACK MAMBA

very strong and fast-acting. And it doesn't just bite once, but strikes repeatedly. If you were bitten, it would be lights out for you very quickly.

This potentially dangerous serpent, which lives in Africa, can slither along the ground at nearly ten miles per hour. That's fast for a snake! It's also lightning quick when it strikes its prey. This amazing hunter has even been known to grab birds and bats right out of the air. Now that's what I call fast food!

TIMBER RATTLESNAKE

Many snakes have ways of warning you to stay away. The timber rattler and other rattlesnakes are among the best at sending a clear signal to back off.

At the end of a rattler's tail is a rattle made of empty segments of dead skin. The rattle grows a bit bigger each time the snake sheds its skin. When the snake shakes its tail, the rattle makes a loud clattering sound that's hard to ignore. The message? "Don't bother me—unless you want to feel my fangs!"

TIMBER RATTLESNAKE

Timber rattlers can grow to between three and five feet long, and are found throughout the United States.

Like other rattlesnakes, timber rattlers have sense organs on their faces for detecting heat. They're called heat pits. These special organs "see" heat, the way eyes see light. They help the rattler find its prey—even in the dark.

Don't be surprised if you come across this snake in your history books. Over two hundred years ago, America fought a war of independence against the British. When they won the war, Americans created signs and flags showing the timber rattlesnake. The flags said, "Don't tread on me." Like the snake's rattle, the symbol sent a message to the British. "Don't bother me!"

DONT TREAD ON ME

TIMBER RATTLESNAKE

GREEN ANACONDA

In this corner, the heavyweight champion of the snake world—the green anaconda!

Weighing in at over five hundred pounds, the green anaconda is the heaviest snake in the world. It's also one of the longest. Most grow to just over sixteen feet in length. But some have been found that were nearly thirty feet long! Can you imagine a snake that weighs as much as two football players and is as long as your school bus? That's a whole lot of snake!

This giant is very strong, with a thick, muscular body. Believe me—I know how powerful they are! I saw my first green anaconda in Ecuador, South America. It was lying on a tree branch hanging over a river. It weighed eighty pounds and was as long as the canoe we were in. I nearly tipped the boat trying to get it down!

GREEN ANACONDA

Although large anacondas can travel on land, they move much better in water. So they spend a lot of time in the swamps and waterways of the South American rainforests where they live.

The green anaconda hides in the water to surprise its prey. With its brownish green skin and dark spots, the anaconda is well camouflaged and very hard to see underwater.

The anaconda isn't venomous, but it is a *constrictor*. That means it uses its strength to capture and kill its prey. When dinner comes along, the huge snake grabs its victim with its mouth and body. Then it wraps itself around the animal and squeezes so hard that the creature can't breathe.

What's on the menu for an anaconda? How about deer, *capybara* (large South American rodents), birds, and lizards. There's also *caiman* (alligator-like reptiles called crocodilians) and crocodiles. When you're a heavyweight snake, you have a heavyweight appetite!

ANACONDA CONSTRICTING A HERON

RETICULATED PYTHON

The reticulated python is a large, powerful snake that lives in the rainforests of Southeast Asia. It may not be the heaviest snake, but it *is* the longest. Most adult reticulated pythons grow to over sixteen feet in length. The longest ones grow to over thirty feet!

As you might have guessed, a snake this size has a pretty big appetite. It eats birds and large mammals, like pigs and deer. Like all pythons, the reticulated python is able to find its prey using its heat pits.

RETICULATED PYTHON

When the python's prey gets close enough, the snake strikes with its powerful jaws. It holds the prey using its long teeth. Then it coils its muscular body around the struggling creature, squeezing until the animal can't breathe anymore.

ROCK PYTHON CONSTRICTING A GAZELLE

Like many large snakes, a reticulated python can open its jaws surprisingly wide—wide enough to get a whole deer into its mouth. Then it swallows its dinner—fur, hoofs, bones, and all!

Reticulated pythons do something that most snakes don't. Most snakes abandon their eggs once they're laid. But when a

RETICULATED PYTHON FEEDING ON A DEER

female reticulated python lays its eggs, it coils around them. Then it quivers its muscles over and over again. This "shivering" heats up the snake's body, which keeps the eggs warm and helps them hatch.

RETICULATED PYTHON WARMING HER EGGS

Now that you've gotten to know snakes better, I hope you'll want to learn even more about them!

TWO-HEADED KINGSNAKE

I go on trips around the world to study snakes. But you just have to visit your local library, museum, or zoo. You could also join a *herpetological* club near you. (Herpetology is the study of reptiles and amphibians.)

You could even see if any snakes live near you! And, with the help of your parents, who knows? You could be the one going on the next great snake expedition! Good luck!